D0922849

Our House Is
in this Section
But it doesn't
Seem Like Home
Without YouAll

here

Love
John

THE FAN

BY THOMAS F. HALE

WRITTEN BY BILL WESTBROOK

PHOTOGRAPHED
DESIGNED
AND PUBLISHED BY
HALE PUBLISHING

First Printing 1972
Second Printing 1975

Copyright ©1972 by Thomas F. Hale
First Edition Library of Congress Catalogue
Card Number 72-91745
All rights reserved

This book, or parts thereof, must not be
reproduced in any form without written
permission from Thomas F. Hale.

Printed by W.M. Brown & Son, Inc.
Richmond, Virginia.

Our sincere gratitude to the many Fan residents who graciously allowed us access to their homes and their thoughts. To the Valentine Museum and the Fan District Association, our thanks for assistance and encouragement.

Foreword

The Fan is an idea of living.

That idea is formed somewhere within these pages, more from our feelings than outright facts. Regretfully, there are so many photographs we didn't have pages for, so many paragraphs that could be expanded into books.

But the essence of the Fan is here. A sense of its being; what it has been; what it can become.

For all that it is, the Fan is not by itself. Across America there are similar areas where people are exploring the potential of old neighborhoods and putting together a new concept of living. In the process they create a sense of identity and, consequently, a source of pride.

Every homeowner who has ever tried to renovate a house, organize a neighborhood meeting, plan a park and fight City Hall all at the same time knows the feeling.

This book is really their testimony that it can be done.

The sun rises and brings morning up the streets.

Gas park lamps are through for the night. There is a hazed hushness, just an instant, and the first car starts the day.

The first dog takes a walk.

Slowly the subtleties are present if you care to be aware of them. College students going to classes, going through your neighborhood and through your life.

Work traffic.

Bicycles in ones and twos, weaving in and out and around cars that aren't awake yet.

Parks with their morning babies.

Doors opening onto stoops with new papers and hands coming out of cracks to find them.

You are into the morning in the Fan. And you are conscious of experiencing others' activities.

The Fan is a distinctly urban idea of day-to-day living in a door-to-door neighborhood. Where life is immediate to your senses. And you are aware of the currency of things around you.

People involved in the moment. As they are involved in the city. And involved in the neighborhood.

It is a renaissance of city living back to a time when the city offered more promises than problems. When the cultural pace of the day was set along the shady, crooked streets lined with gracious Victorian houses. And a prize garden earned its proud owner near immortality in the neighborhood.

The revitalization is taking things back and moving things forward in the Fan District. There is a population here of about 20,000 persons in an area of roughly a square mile near downtown Richmond, Virginia, and adjacent to Virginia Commonwealth University.

To the north, the Fan District is bordered by historic Monument Avenue; to the east by Monroe Park; to the south by Floyd Avenue; and to the west by the Boulevard.

The history of the land and the streets that cross it reaches far back into Virginia's past.

An early historical sketch of the area gives an accounting of a short but sharp action between the British and American troops near a spot bounded today by Laurel Street to Cherry Street, and Floyd Avenue to Park Avenue. On that spot stood an old tavern and a settlement of small houses which, supposedly, was afterwards known as Scuffle Towne because of the strenuous battle that occurred that day.

Another tale suggests that the name Scuffles was given to the tavern by the owner, Mr. Richard Reins, because of his difficulties in getting to Richmond from the small eighteenth century community.

The sign outside the tavern read, "Help a Fellow Scuffler Through," and the mint juleps Mr. Reins served inside were often found to be all the help a traveler needed. The tavern was still standing and serving until 1912, when it was demolished.

The road to Richmond was known as Scuffle Towne Road until its name was changed to Park Avenue when Monroe Park became part of the city in 1867.

As late as 1851, the park was a field of wild blackberry bushes inhabited by an old Negro woman who was reputed to be a former slave of John B. Harvie, a Colonel of Virginia Militia in 1776. Colonel Harvie was later to become Registrar of the Land Office and mayor of the city. Harvie Street in the Fan bears his name today.

Not far from Harvie Street stands the monument to General Robert E. Lee. It was unveiled on May 29, 1890 in what was then an open field, the nearest house being over 300 yards away. Over 25,000 people, many of whom were Confederate veterans, paraded past the statue that day.

The War Between the States gave the South other heroes, and Richmond other monuments and other street names. One boulevard in particular, Monument Avenue, is perhaps the most famous thoroughfare in Richmond. The Lee statue is located along this avenue today, and also the monument to Jefferson Davis, the President of the Confederacy. Davis stands near the site of an important gun placement needed to protect the city from a westward attack during the four years of the siege.

Other monuments pay tribute to Stonewall Jackson, J.E.B. Stuart and, farther westward along the avenue, Matthew Fontaine Maury, who was called the "Pathfinder of the Seas." It was the proposal for monuments to Stuart and Davis which occasioned the name change from what was then Franklin Street to Monument Avenue in 1906.

The Civil War prompted the change from Federal Avenue to Floyd Avenue as well, for obvious reasons.

Addison Street was formerly called Strawberry Street because of the wild strawberries that grew in the fields nearby.

Hanover Avenue was named for a rascal of a King, George I of England. He was born May 28, 1660 in Hanover, Germany and chiefly distinguished himself as a ruler by taking mistresses like most people take aspirin today. Often, and two at a time.

Around the turn of the twentieth century, the streets bulged with traffic during a boom time in Richmond's history. Tobacco was king and Richmond was a kingdom of growers.

Later, when the Depression hit the country in the 1930's, the area lost much of its value. It steadily declined, and the post World War II rush to the suburbs compounded the problem. It was the beginning of the Great Exodus to the ranch-style homes in House & Garden sitting on one-half acre lots, each surrounded by grass and barbecue grills.

In 1941, however, a group called the West Avenue Improvement Association was founded as a pest control agent for the little three-block street. This was probably the first organization of its kind within the area dedicated to the improvement of the neighborhood. The residents have since been dedicated to its growth as well; in fact, the pseudonym "Stork Alley" was bestowed upon the street for producing more children in a three-block area than probably any other such avenue in the world.

To a large extent, the West Avenue Association continues to manage its own affairs today. The residents elect their own mayor, conduct annual tours and clean-up drives; and it's probably still true that if "Old Dame Rumor" arrives on the street too scantily clad, she's always dressed in the finest embroidery before she leaves.

This was the beginning of a group feeling or attitude about a part of the area now called The Fan. Actual revitalization began in a substantial way about 1950. Young people began moving into the old homes and taking a chance on the less prestigious neighborhood. Older residents, for whom the area had special meaning because of strong family ties, watched the new faces on their old streets increase.

As renewed interest in the area grew, so did an obvious need for some kind of association that could speak for the neighborhood as a whole. A group that could be a voice for the betterment of the entire area by virtue of the fact that its members shared a common denominator: they lived in the Fan District.

Thus, on October 12, 1961, The Fan District Association of Richmond, Virginia was formed. Its overall purpose was, and still is, to preserve and enhance the character of the neighborhood. And its membership has grown in recent years to over 600 families.

The Fan District Association continues to be the focus of direction for the neighborhood as a whole. Yet special interest groups, such as the several organizations formed to preserve the character of Monument Avenue, are important political voices as well. The results of their work have often been dramatic. A drive down Monument Avenue over paving blocks instead of asphalt is a reminder that battles against "progress" can be won.

Largely because of the efforts of the Fan District Association and these active groups, the Fan has never been more alive with possibilities and enthusiasm than now. On block after block, Fan residents are planning a neighborhood environment where the individual can be what he is, or wants to be. Where one contributes to the whole but is not patterned after the mass.

Typically, the styles of renovation mirror the many kinds of people in the neighborhood. But there are still basic similarities in the big two- and three-story townhouses.

Wide pine floors can be found in most of them, often in entry halls big enough to roller skate in. Floor and ceiling moldings with intricate detail outline the interiors.

Fireplaces with carved mantels and marble hearths burn brightly in bedrooms and dining rooms, just as in living rooms. And every room seems spacious, with ceilings so high that the top doesn't have to be cut off the Christmas tree, even if it's 10 feet tall.

There is a common feeling down each street in the neighborhood. Somehow it exists. Perhaps created by the closeness of the houses. There is surely a closeness among the people.

And they are so unalike.

Doctors, lawyers, elected city officials, artists, students, clerks, contractors, small shop owners, factory workers, teachers.

One lives around the corner and up the block from the other.

Living amongst the variance gives one a unique perspective on living itself. For, while people are different in their life styles, there is a mutual harmony of independence in the Fan. Residents are somehow in common by the uncommonness of it all.

Homes on this scale,
with this kind of craftsmanship
and detail, aren't being built
anymore. But they are rapidly
being bought and renovated.

And always, the work is hard
to make the living easy.

Projects sit on top of projects.
A good plumber's name is holy
next to you-know-whose. And
up and down the streets the
word is all about what so-and-
so is doing.

Homes that begin with identical
floor plans are renovated to be
worlds apart.

Contemporary here resides
next to seventeenth century
colonial there. Spanish
haciendas softly lit by thick-
scented candles face Tudor
cottages with quaint square
panes and carriage houses in
the back.

The homes of the Fan date to the 1880's, and the architecture is really a mixed bag of influences. Georgian, Victorian, Italian, Spanish, Colonial, Tudor and others.

Early contractors even mixed different styles within the design of a single house. Thus there is a legacy of Italian arcades and porches rimmed with Victorian iron fringe-work; Georgian entry halls bathed in stained glass light.

On the fringe and
side streets the block improve-
ments are coming; the projects.
There are boarded-up houses
still. Gray, peeling, painted
walls waiting for an idea.

Here, there is a
feeling of almost super privacy
within the homes. A womb-
feeling. You close the door and
turn off the outside world with
a flick of a light switch.

Your children come inside
to play. Because sometimes it's
not safe outside. The price of
uptown living is uptown traffic
and crime. So the children of the
Fan learn to cope with
reality early.

There is the diversity of people
in the neighborhood. (Where
else would you find two children
on the same street named
Sacha?)

Transients coming through at
odd hours.

There is city dirt that doesn't
just brush off. And city noise,
although somehow it becomes
silent after awhile.

There's "yellow thing" park,
and "the wall" for tennis.
There are sidewalk games and
small backyards not big enough
for football but perfect for
other things.

Because every child makes his
own playground. Special and
very natural for him.

No doubt living in the Fan has made parents closer to their children. More attention is given to where they are, what they're doing. There are trips to museums and to park concerts, to explore the city libraries and to take advantage of the many plays, classes and offerings of the university.

Increasingly, the university plays a major role in the life of the Fan.

Children grow into adults in four years there. And the process scares hell out of many residents around the neighborhood along with parents around the country.

But the university is a force of change within the Fan. What it gives is vitality. Intellectual stimulation. A forum for ideas. And what it takes is some getting used to by many more conservative, more traditional residents.

When braless, barefoot girls start walking through your life, it makes you realize that some social changes deserve a second look. No matter how tradition bound you are.

When there are jam sessions from balconies overlooking elderly residents in tea gardens, you learn to tap your foot to the beat of a different drum.

The dress and color of the university students contribute to the attitude of individuality in the Fan. There is a contrast in life styles between youth and over-thirty old age. It mixes and provides a kind of ferment that makes life more interesting for both.

There are students boarding throughout the Fan. Mansions have been turned into dormitories, in some cases, to accommodate them. And, in some cases, mansions which long ago would have been razed have been saved.

In addition, the growth of the university has kept out encroaching commercialism at the lower end of the Fan. In many ways, it has made the Fan a small college town.

And if the residents enjoy the university, the students enjoy the unique environment of the Fan. There are cobbled alleys and yard sales and parks for rock concerts. There are grand weddings and simple celebrations to commemorate past history. And there are tours to bring the students inside the life here even more. At garden time. And especially Christmas time.

In the spirit of the season mixed with a little old fashioned showing-off, the Fan opens its doors for Christmas.

There are homemade decorations. And recipes that pass across back fences into warm kitchens next door.

There are cocktail parties on every street. And visitors drive the curve of Park into the candles flickering in the windows.

There is a Williamsburg quaintness and traditionalism.

And all the things that infuse the Fan with warmth are somehow made brighter in the crackling fire of a sitting room.

This is Christmas in the Fan; and yet, the day after Christmas you haven't lost much.

The mornings still begin the same way. The traffic noise. People moving through.

Familiar shops open their doors. Landmarks of the neighborhood.

The Fan is a small-town community surrounded by city steel and superstructure; everyone is a part and it is a part of all. The work of the Fan Association is to keep that small-town feeling alive. Keep it from being swallowed by the city.

So the Fan Association politics for parks. And parking. And protection from the kind of big city dehumanization and decay that sends people flying to their city-limit living and shopping center suburbs.

They are people with a plan. It is a Master Plan to create and hold an ideal living environment. Recognizing that the city proper must govern growth and improvement within municipal sections, the Fan Association is attempting to merge the Master Plan with the city's plan for the future. And in the process redefine what a community can do to influence its own destiny.

The Master Plan asks for block core parks for the families in the Fan.

The concept of the parks is to transform unsightly or neglected land in the interior of the blocks into play areas for children.

The forgotten, fallen-down garages and abandoned side lots now only hint of the possibilities they hold. Imagination can make them brightly lit little parks, landscaped with shrubbery and benches and children's sand boxes.

And, eventually, the neighborhood could be a series of parks interconnected by walkways and bicycle paths in and around residences.

The Master Plan asks for rezoning to prevent the big, old homes from becoming big, new businesses.

For more owner-occupied residences and fewer personnel-occupied offices.

For segregated commercialism. So that small shops can face other stores and shops across the street. And residents won't have to face the decline of a fine old block because it was good for business.

The Master Plan asks for parking privileges without parking lots. Because as through traffic continues to grow, street space continues to grow less. To create public parking facilities would jeopardize the identity of the neighborhood. The alternative is to restrict parking in some areas of the Fan to neighborhood residents.

The Master Plan asks that underutilized land in the Fan be approved for development as parks, townhouse "courts" or for off-street resident parking. So that the value of housing investments can grow. Along with the value of living in those investments.

And the Master Plan seeks for Fan residents the right to feel free from personal threat to health and safety. There are jokes among Fan residents about "muggy nights out" that have nothing to do with the weather. Maybe there is more crime here in a city neighborhood, or maybe it's just magnified by the closeness the families feel to each other.

But with better street lighting and protection, with less traffic and fewer abandoned structures, there will be fewer problems.

The idea of the Fan can continue to find reality as residents explore the potential that attracted them to the neighborhood in the first place. Potential that will attract new people tomorrow.

They will come because of what they have heard. Perhaps for convenient access to the city. Or to make an investment in grand homes with rapidly increasing values. Or because they believe the neighborhood has a "thing" about it that sets it apart.

Those who come will be cognizant of the problems but fully aware of the opportunities.

Not everyone will stay. But those who do will find a warmth here that perhaps was missing for them in the suburbs. They will find a privacy for their thoughts and lives they've never experienced before.

The Fan is a neighborhood with integrity, created by the people who breathe life into the old townhouses with their time and their money and their resources.

They breed a contagious loyalty that finds its strength in preserving a little uniqueness in a world filled with compromise.

The obvious uniqueness of the Fan, the gracious townhouse living, the curving, shaded streets and the familiar landmarks must obviously be preserved. But there are a thousand details to the Fan's identity that go unnoticed by many who do not live here, or are taken for granted by many that do.

If the Fan is to approach an ideal living environment, as the Master Plan foresees, then all that is unique in the Fan must be preserved. New changes must reflect the existing character of the neighborhood.

The sign of our times does not have to be neon. The light of our lives does not have to be mercury vapor.

To suggest suburban values and artifacts for the Fan is to ignore the broader social value in a cohesive, functioning social unit with a distinct identity.

To alter that identity in the name of "progress" is to miss the most important point to be made about the Fan.

Progress is already here.